AF273194

All the Water on
EARTH

For Amy and Oliver, who are always willing to splash in the waves with me — R.S.

To my nephew, Lawson Goodnight, and all kids that jump in puddles, swim in pools, splash through rivers and drink water every day. It's so important to respect and love this beautiful earth we live on — we only get one! — M.G.

CitizenKid™ is a trademark of Kids Can Press Ltd.

Text © 2026 Rochelle Strauss
Illustrations © 2026 Madelyn Goodnight

All rights reserved. No part of this publication may be reproduced, stored in a retrieval system or transmitted, in any form or by any means, without the prior written permission of Kids Can Press Ltd. or, in case of photocopying or other reprographic copying, a license from The Canadian Copyright Licensing Agency (Access Copyright). For an Access Copyright license, visit www.accesscopyright.ca or call toll free to 1-800-893-5777.

No AI training. Any use of this publication to train generative artificial intelligence (AI) technologies is expressly prohibited.

Published in Canada and the U.S. by Kids Can Press Ltd.
25 Dockside Drive, Toronto, ON M5A 0B5

Kids Can Press is a Corus Entertainment Inc. company

www.kidscanpress.com

The artwork in this book was rendered using mixed media traditional materials (graphite, watercolor paper and colored pencils), and then completed using digital painting software. The text is set in Albert Sans.

Edited by Mary Beth Leatherdale and Kathleen Keenan
Designed by Marie Bartholomew

Printed and bound in Buji, Shenzhen, China, in 8/2025 by WKT Company

CM 26 0 9 8 7 6 5 4 3 2 1

MIX
Paper | Supporting responsible forestry
FSC
www.fsc.org
FSC® C010256

Library and Archives Canada Cataloguing in Publication

Title: All the water on Earth / written by Rochelle Strauss ; illustrated by Madelyn Goodnight.

Names: Strauss, Rochelle, 1967– author | Goodnight, Madelyn, illustrator

Series: CitizenKid.

Description: Series statement: CitizenKid | Includes bibliographical references.

Identifiers: Canadiana (print) 20250204401 | Canadiana (ebook) 2025020441X | ISBN 9781525310881 (hardcover) | ISBN 9781525314872 (EPUB)

Subjects: LCSH: Water — Juvenile literature. | LCSH: Hydrologic cycle — Juvenile literature. | LCSH: Water conservation — Juvenile literature.

Classification: LCC GB662.3 .S77 2026 | DDC j553.7 — dc23

Kids Can Press gratefully acknowledges that the land on which our office is located is the traditional territory of many nations, including the Mississaugas of the Credit, the Anishnabeg, the Chippewa, the Haudenosaunee and the Wendat Peoples, and is now home to many diverse First Nations, Inuit and Métis Peoples.

We thank the Government of Ontario, through Ontario Creates and the Ontario Arts Council; the Canada Council for the Arts; and the Government of Canada, for their financial support of our publishing activity.

All the Water on EARTH

Written by Rochelle Strauss
Illustrated by Madelyn Goodnight

A collection of books that
inform children about the world
and inspire them to be engaged
global citizens

Kids Can Press

If you look closely, you will see.
Water is flowing all around you.

Water ripples through lakes and rivers, inviting you for a dip on a warm summer's day.
It bubbles its way through streams and brooks.

And though you may not see it, water trickles in underground rivers beneath your feet.

Frothy ocean waves crash against the shore,

while icy water sits frozen in glaciers and icebergs.

Fresh ice on a pond invites you for a wintry skate.

Water drizzles down as rain, and pools in puddles all around you, splishing and splashing as you stomp about!

Sparkly white snow swirls around in
blustery blizzards and collects in drifts
along the ground. Hurray, a snow day!

Tiny water droplets shimmer in the morning dew and hang heavy in the evening fog.

There's even water in the air you breathe ... and in the steam rising from your mug of hot cocoa.

There's water in every plant and animal, including you. Because people are animals, too! There's so much water all around you that from space, Earth looks blue.

Water is always on the move. It circles from Earth
to the sky and back down again ... over and over and over.
Gaze up at the clouds, and you will see water moving
through the sky and around the planet, too.

All water on Earth is connected. Every lake, stream, pond or river is joined together. This means the water you use in your home ...

... is the same water that a person in Kenya might get from a well and the same water that someone in India might collect from a river. It's even the same water that plants and animals all over the world drink, swim or live in.

For millions of years, the amount of water on Earth has been the same. There's no more water now than when the dinosaurs roamed the planet. Imagine ... the water you sipped today may be the same water a triceratops slurped!

And there will be no more water on Earth ten years from now.

Or one hundred.

Or one thousand.

Or even one million.

Because all the water on Earth is ... all the water on Earth.

All living things on Earth need water to survive. Every plant and animal — even you!

But not all water is the same. Salt water churns in the ocean and all the seas. Splashing ocean waves leave a salty taste on your lips.

Fresh water fills lakes, rivers, ponds and your water bottle when you are thirsty.

With more and more people living on Earth, we use more fresh water today than ever before.

27

Boiling hot water cooks up pasta for supper, then soapy water scrubs the pot clean.

Water sprays from a farmer's hose, helping her grow food to feed people all over the world.

The energy of rushing water is captured
to create the electricity needed to power
some cities and homes.

Nearly everything you see was made using water.

Water made the pages of this book. And the ink. It made the clothes you wear and the bike you ride. Water also made the glass you drink your water from!

Water even carries the cargo ships that sail around the world, delivering these things to people like you and me.

Some countries have plenty of fresh water, and most people have water flowing through pipes in their homes.

But other countries have very little, and people must walk a long way to get the water they need.

You and I and every living species on Earth need clean water. But not all the water on Earth is clean.

Rain washes pollution from the land into rivers and streams. People also dump waste into the water.

Polluted water is dangerous for people to drink. It poisons plants and animals and harms habitats, too.

Sometimes there just isn't enough clean water to go around ... no matter where you live.

Earth needs our help to protect all the water. And thankfully, people all over the world are working together to make sure there's enough clean water for all life on Earth.

Because no matter where it's found, and no matter what form it takes, all the water on Earth is ... all the water on Earth.

Author's Note

My most favorite place to be is near, in, or on the water! I love swimming in lakes, kayaking on rivers and snorkeling in the sea. I love sailing on boats, looking for whales, searching for creatures in tide pools, and sitting on shorelines listening to the crashing waves. But water is more than just where you and I play.

Water is the most important thing on Earth. Water quenches our thirst and grows our food. It's where plants, animals and tiny organisms, such as bacteria and amoebas live. We travel on water, and water travels through our bodies and the bodies of other living species.

We share this planet with about eight billion people. We also share it with millions and millions of animals, plants and other organisms, too! We all need water to survive. But around the world, not everyone has access to water. Some places have lots of water. Others very little. And some water, and watery habitats, are polluted.

Water moves around the planet in a loop called the water cycle. It evaporates from the ocean, lakes and rivers, and travels to the sky as steam. There it cools and changes into the tiny water droplets that make clouds. As the droplets get heavier, they fall back down to Earth as rain or snow. Water loops through the water cycle over and over again. But the water cycle is a closed system — which means Earth can never get more water!

That's why it's important to protect the water on Earth. So all of Earth's inhabitants have access to clean water, no matter where they live. And you can help! You and your family can use less water around your home, or collect litter to protect waterways, or speak up about water conservation. There are so many ways to protect Earth's water. Another way to protect water is to learn more about it. And one of the best ways to do that is to get outside! Explore your local waterways and investigate all the species that live there. See for yourself all the things that water is and does.

Remember, all the water on Earth is ... all the water on Earth!

Let's Talk

1. Where do you find water? What watery places are your favorite? Why?

2. Can you name the three different states that water comes in? How is water different in each state?

3. What are some of the different ways you use water every day?

4. Imagine that all the water you had for the day filled just one bucket. How would you use water differently? What things might you choose to do without?

5. Why is access to clean water important for people? Why is it important for all living things?

6. Water conservation means protecting all the water on Earth. What ideas do you have, or what actions can you take, to protect or conserve water — at home and at school?

Dear Reader,

We hope that this book has sparked thoughtful questions and inspirational conversations about what it means to make a difference.

Developed by Kids Can Press, the CitizenKid collection encourages young readers to learn about global issues and then think about ways that they can help improve the communities they live in, and the world at large.

Almost 2 million CitizenKid books have been sold to date, and the collection has been translated into over 25 languages. CitizenKid books have garnered worldwide critical acclaim.

Each CitizenKid book is developed with one or more of the United Nations Sustainable Development Goals (SDG) in mind, such as climate action, clean water and sanitation, gender equality, poverty and more. The Goals are a universal call to action to end poverty, protect the planet and improve the lives and prospects of everyone, everywhere.

For our part, Kids Can Press is a proud signatory of the UN's SDG Publisher's Compact. The Compact is designed to accelerate progress to achieve the Goals through publishing books that support positive change.

How will you help change the world?

#CitizenKid

Discover More

- All-Atlantic Blue Schools Network: https://allatlanticblueschools.com.

- Clendenan, Megan. *Fresh Air, Clean Water: Our Right to a Healthy Environment.* Orca Books, 2022.

- EARTHDAY.ORG: https://www.earthday.org.

- Earth Rangers: https://www.earthrangers.com.

- Hughes, Susan. *Walking for Water: How One Boy Stood Up for Gender Equality.* Kids Can Press, 2021.

- Indigenous STEAM: https://indigenoussteam.org.

- Jane Goodall Institute Roots and Shoots: https://rootsandshoots.global.

- Marshall, Elder Albert D., and Louise Zimanyi. *Walking Together.* Annick Press, 2023.

- Ocean Week Canada Blue Learning Lab: https://oceanweekcan.ca/blue-learning-lab/.

- Project WET: https://www.projectwet.org.

- Robertson, Joanne. *The Water Walker.* Second Story Press, 2017.

- Strauss, Rochelle. *One Well: The Story of Water on Earth.* Kids Can Press, 2007.

- Strauss, Rochelle. *The Global Ocean.* Kids Can Press, 2022.

- United Nations Sustainable Development Goals: https://sdgs.un.org/goals.

- United Nations — World Water Day: https://www.worldwaterday.org.